WORKBOOK CONTENTS

PART I: BE YOU. BE FEARLESS.

PART II: TRANSFORM LIVES

D1402822

WE'RE *unstoppable* INFLUENCERS...
WE SHARE OUR GOD-GIVEN GIFTS WITH THE WORLD.
WE'RE EXPERTS IN OUR FIELDS. WE'RE ON A MISSION TO
POSITIVELY   SO COME ALONG FOR THE RIDE,
INFLUENCE PEOPLE'S LIVES. **OR GET OUT OF OUR WAY!**
WE'RE COMMITTED TO EXPANDING OUR SPHERE
OF INFLUENCE SO WE CAN MAKE A BIG IMPACT.
WE INSPIRE AND UPLIFT OTHERS DAILY.
WE'RE PERFECTLY IMPERFECT. WE TACKLE FEAR AND SELF-DOUBT
LIKE A *boss.* WE DON'T LET OUR LIGHT DIM,
EVEN IN THE WINDS OF ADVERSITY.
WE WEAR THE ARMOR OF OUR TRUTH AND
EQUIP OURSELVES WITH **TOOLS** AND **LESSONS**
THAT ALLOW OUR LIGHT TO SHINE BRIGHT,
NO MATTER WHAT. WE ARE NOT VICTIMS.
WE'RE ETERNAL STUDENTS
LOOKING FOR THE LESSONS GIFTED TO US IN CHALLENGES.
WE'RE   WE DO THE WORK WE'RE INTENDED TO DO
ACTION   AND MAKE NO EXCUSES. WE KNOW THAT TO
TAKERS   UNLEASH OUR INFLUENCE IN THE WORLD, WE
MUST STEP OUTSIDE OUR COMFORT ZONE.
WE HAVE FAITH, AND WE'LL DO THINGS EVEN WHEN WE'RE SCARED.
WE USE OUR INFLUENCE FOR *good*
WE KNOW OUR WORTH AND CHARGE ACCORDINGLY.
WE KNOW THAT BY SHARING OUR GIFTS WITH THE WORLD,
WE'LL HAVE EVERYTHING WE WANT IN LIFE.
IF YOU WANT TO JOIN OUR MOVEMENT, ONE DECISION
IS ALL IT TAKES—THE DECISION TO LIVE LIFE AS AN
UNSTOPPABLE INFLUENCER.

UNSTOPPABLE · INFLUENCE ·

UNSTOPPABLEINFLUENCE.COM

UNSTOPPABLE
INFLUENCE

Companion Workbook

Hi Fellow Influencer!

I have created this Companion Workbook for you to use in conjunction with my book *Unstoppable Influence: Be You. Be Fearless. Transform Lives.*

The Workbook by itself doesn't cover all of the exercises, tips, strategies and secrets that can transform your life and business, so if you don't already own the book visit www.UnstoppableInfluence.com to get your copy now so you can learn how to discover your gifts and unleash your influence in the world!

Here are a few tips to get the most out of this Companion Workbook.

- Many people find they get more out of the actual book if they read it from cover to cover first, *then* go back to the beginning and complete the exercises chapter by chapter. Other people prefer to begin reading and feel prompted to do certain exercises immediately. Others go one step at a time and do each exercise before moving onto the next chapter. I encourage you to just do what feels right for YOU.

- No matter how you do it, I do encourage you to complete ALL the exercises, whether it takes you 30 days, 6 months or a year. If you are committed to discovering and fulfilling your calling, this will be a vital part of your journey to Unstoppable Influence.

- **Be honest**. The whole point of working through this workbook is so you can see where you are now and how you are growing and changing. You are perfectly imperfect. Commit to unpeeling the onion and discovering your naked Truth.

- Not every chapter in this workbook has an exercise. If I felt the book said it all, I didn't include an exercise. However, I have included space for you to record your aha moments, inspiration and ideas for each chapter.

If my book has had a profound impact on your life, I want to hear from you! Email me at natasha@UnstoppableInfluence.com. Above all, I hope that you LOVE the book, LOVE the workbook, and LOVE your journey to Unstoppable Influence.

With Love,
Natasha

PART I

BE YOU.
BE FEARLESS.

WHAT IS UNSTOPPABLE INFLUENCE?

"This little light of mine, I'm going to let it shine.

Let it shine! Let it shine! Let it shine!

Ev'ry where I go, I'm going to let it shine!

Oh, ev'ry where I go, I'm going to let it shine!"

~ "THIS LITTLE LIGHT OF MINE" (HARRY DIXON LOES)

2

LIVING A LIFE BY DESIGN, NOT DEFAULT

Twenty years from now you will be more disappointed by the things you didn't do, than by the things you did.

~ MARK TWAIN

ARE YOU CURRENTLY LIVING LIFE BY DESIGN OR BY DEFAULT? IF YOU'RE LIVING LIFE BY DEFAULT, IDENTIFY 3-5 THINGS YOU CAN DO OVER THE NEXT 90 DAYS TO GET OUT OF THE RUT AND BACK INTO ALIGNMENT WITH YOUR PURPOSE?

3

MY JOURNEY TO BECOMING AN UNSTOPPABLE INFLUENCER

> *"I know for sure: Your journey begins with a choice to get up, step out, and live fully."*
>
> ~ OPRAH WINFREY

Write your story, warts and all, then look for themes and patterns. Let your instinct guide you how far back your story should go. For purposes of this exercise, you want the words to flow, so allow yourself to write without editing.

Now that you've written your story, re-read it. What lessons have you learned that can help others on their paths? Write those lessons below.

4

HOW TO BECOME UNSTOPPABLE

"The question isn't who is going to let me;

it's who is going to stop me."

~ AYN RAND

PRAY OR MEDITATE ON THE INTENDED SCOPE OF YOUR INFLUENCE. WHAT IS THE SCOPE OF YOUR INFLUENCE?

THE UNSTOPPABLE INFLUENCER PLEDGE

I will share my gifts with the world. I commit to expanding my sphere of influence so I can make a big impact. I will inspire and uplift others daily. I will tackle fear and self-doubt like a BOSS.

I will not let my light dim, even in the winds of adversity. I will wear the armor of Truth and equip myself with tools and lessons that allow my light to shine bright, NO MATTER WHAT.

I will take action and do the work I'm intended to do. I will not make excuses. I will step outside my comfort zone and do things even when I'm scared.

I will use my influence for GOOD. I know my worth and will charge accordingly.

I am an Unstoppable Influencer.

_____   _____
Date   Signature

CONGRATULATIONS!

NOW THAT YOU'VE SIGNED THE PLEDGE, GO TO UNSTOPPABLEINFLUENCE.COM/GROUP AND JOIN OUR UNSTOPPABLE INFLUENCER COMMUNITY. INTRODUCE YOURSELF, AND BOLDLY DECLARE YOUR COMMITMENT TO SHARING YOUR GIFT WITH THE WORLD. (BONUS POINTS IF YOU DO IT ON A VIDEO!)

5

UNBECOMING

"Maybe the journey isn't so much about becoming anything. Maybe it's about un-becoming everything that isn't really you so you can be who you were meant to be in the first place."

~ UNKNOWN

As you read Chapter 5, some memories were likely triggered. Write them down here. How have these memories had a positive or negative impact on your light?

TRUTH TIME! PRAY OR MEDITATE ON THE AREAS WHERE YOU MAY BE BLOCKED. THEN, LIST ALL OF THE MENTAL GARBAGE THAT NEEDS TO BE RELEASED TO BEGIN YOUR PROCESS OF UNBECOMING.

ENERGY CLEARING:

What is It?

Have you ever woken up ready to conquer the world, motivated, and full of energy only to walk into the office or get on a phone call and suddenly feel like you're being weighed down by a ton of bricks?

Has your mood ever gone from good to bad or from calm to stressed without anything *really* happening yet?

Have you ever entered a room thinking, "she must have had a rough morning"?

If you're like me, the answer is *yes*. That's because we are all energetically connected. This, in combination with your life experiences and the demands placed upon you, makes it easy to feel depleted and out of balance. At times, you may feel stunned or stuck, unsure of which direction to go next. In these scenarios, energy clearing and balancing sessions can be beneficial. These sessions help re-align all aspects of YOU, the mind, body, and spirit.

An energy clearing and balancing session removes energy that no longer serves you or the greater good, replenishes depleted energy, and brings balance and harmony to the body which supports the body's natural healing processes.

These sessions do not require anything of you except to relax while laying down fully clothed on a massage table and being open to receiving the healing life force energy. The practitioner is the conduit for the energy to flow and will touch certain points on your body for this to take place. Most often, you will feel a sense of relaxation and you might experience other physical sensations like a warmth or coolness move through your body, other times you may not feel anything at all which is okay too.

Like an onion, we have layers that are being peeled away as we are *unbecoming* and for some people it may take more than one session to find the clarity and balance they are longing for and for others, one time may be sufficient. The beauty in these sessions is there is nothing to lose since your body receives what it needs most at that moment in time. Many energy medicine practitioners offer remote sessions as well where you can be in the comfort of your own home.

Want more? https://www.UnstoppableInfluence.com/Energy

EMOTION CODE:

What is It?

Emotionally-charged events from your past can still be haunting you in the form of "trapped emotions"; emotional energies that literally inhabit your body. Trapped emotions can create pain, emotional stress and eventual disease. With a skilled Emotion Code practitioner, you can quickly and easily rid yourself of damaging emotional baggage and "trapped emotions," find and teardown your "Heart-wall" to unlock better health, relationships and abundance.

✧ *The Emotion Code*™ Book:
http://www.drbradleynelson.com/the-emotion-code/

BODY CODE:

What is It?

Developed by Dr. Bradley Nelson, *The Body Code*™ is a cutting-edge energetic healing system. *The Body Code Mind Map System*™ identifies imbalances in the body that can be released or corrected. A Certified Body Code Practitioner will work with you to identify and release/correct imbalances underlying your symptoms of discomfort.

Whether you are dealing with acute or chronic symptoms, or are seeking ways to prevent disease, pain or disability, *The Body Code*™ is a tool for supporting your body, mind and spirit. *The Body Code*™ is not a substitute for standard medical care. It is an adjunct for you to use for the purpose of removing toxic energies that interfere with your body's natural healing abilities.

✧ *The Body Code*™ Book:
http://bodycodehealingsystem.com

✧ Karen Sheeks, RN, MS: Emotion Code & Body Code Certified Practitioner
http://shastalight.com

HYPNOSIS:

https://www.UnstoppableInfluence.com/hypnosis

YOUR NEW LIFE AS AN UNSTOPPABLE INFLUENCER

"There is no passion to be found playing small—in settling for a life that is less than the one you are capable of living."

~ NELSON MANDELA

How you are currently spending your time? Write down your tasks for 3 days.

DAY 1

5 AM	
6 AM	
7 AM	
8 AM	
9 AM	
10 AM	
11 AM	
12 PM	
1 PM	
2 PM	
3 PM	
4 PM	
5 PM	
6 PM	
7 PM	
8 PM	
9 PM	
10 PM	
11 PM	
12 AM	

DAY 2

5 AM	
6 AM	
7 AM	
8 AM	
9 AM	
10 AM	
11 AM	
12 PM	
1 PM	
2 PM	
3 PM	
4 PM	
5 PM	
6 PM	
7 PM	
8 PM	
9 PM	
10 PM	
11 PM	
12 AM	

DAY 3

5 AM	
6 AM	
7 AM	
8 AM	
9 AM	
10 AM	
11 AM	
12 PM	
1 PM	
2 PM	
3 PM	
4 PM	
5 PM	
6 PM	
7 PM	
8 PM	
9 PM	
10 PM	
11 PM	
12 AM	

WHAT DID YOU LEARN FROM WRITING OUT YOUR DAILY ROUTINE FOR 3 DAYS? ARE YOU OPERATING IN ALIGNMENT WITH YOUR DESIRE TO BECOME AN UNSTOPPABLE INFLUENCER AND PLAY A BIGGER GAME? IF NOT, WHAT NEEDS TO BE CHANGED?

LOOK AT YOUR CIRCLE OF INFLUENCE. ARE THE PEOPLE IN YOUR LIFE HELPING YOU MOVE TOWARD FULFILLING YOUR PURPOSE OR PUSHING YOU AWAY FROM IT? LOOK ON YOUR NIGHTSTAND, IN iTUNES, OR ON YOUR KINDLE. ARE THE BOOKS YOU'RE READING AND THE MUSIC YOU'RE LISTENING TO IN ALIGNMENT WITH YOUR CALLING? REFLECT ON WHETHER YOU'RE HAPPY WITH THE WAY YOUR LIFE IS NOW? WHAT CHANGES DO YOU NEED TO MAKE?

WHAT ACTIONS WILL YOU COMMIT TO TAKING IN THE NEXT 30 DAYS TO LIVE IN ALIGNMENT WITH YOUR PURPOSE?

ACTION	DEADLINE	DONE
		❏
		❏
		❏
		❏
		❏
		❏
		❏
		❏
		❏
		❏
		❏
		❏
		❏
		❏
		❏
		❏
		❏
		❏
		❏
		❏

7

CLEARING THE HURDLES TO YOUR INFLUENCE

"In the middle of a difficulty lies opportunity."

~ ALBERT EINSTEIN

Everyone has thoughts they replay over and over again in their minds. What are some potentially unproductive thoughts you repeat to yourself? List them and categorize them as either Ego or Truth.

Unproductive Thought	Ego/Truth
I'm stressed out, so I need a glass of wine.	Ego

THE BUSY BEE TRAP

"Either you run the day or the day runs you."

~ JIM ROHN

Are you taking care of yourself? Use the planner to map out your weekly plan for self care and commit to at least one act of self-care per week!

Self-Care Weekly Planner

Monday	Tuesday	Wednesday	Thursday	Friday	Saturday	Sunday
	Yoga Class			Epsom Salt Bath		Epsom Salt Bath

9

WHAT DO YOU REALLY WANT?

"You are never too old to set another goal or to dream a new dream."

~ C.S. LEWIS

Go to a quiet place. Turn off your phone or any other distractions. Re-read the instructions for this exercise in *Unstoppable Influence* (page 87).

"Who am I without limitations?"

WHERE DO YOU WANT TO BE ON THIS DATE, THREE YEARS FROM NOW?

WHAT DO I HAVE IN MY LIFE BECAUSE I FACE NO LIMITATIONS?

10

DISCOVERING YOUR PURPOSE

> *"The creation of a thousand forests*
>
> *is in one acorn."*
>
> ~ RALPH WALDO EMERSON

Meditate or pray on what you've been called to do. If you have received a calling, write it here.

If you have a calling but haven't acted upon it, reflect on the reasons why and write them down. What mental garbage is preventing you from living your life's purpose?

What are 3-5 actions you can take in the next 30 days to eliminate some of the garbage?

COMMIT TO PARTICIPATING IN AT LEAST THREE EXPERIENCES THAT HAVE THE POTENTIAL TO HELP YOU GROW PERSONALLY OVER THE NEXT THREE MONTHS. *(I.E., GETTING A MASSAGE FOR THE FIRST TIME, SKYDIVING, OR SOMETHING IN BETWEEN…BROWNIE POINTS IF THE EXPERIENCE SCARES THE DAYLIGHTS OUT OF YOU!)*

GROWTH EXPERIENCE	DEADLINE	DONE
		☐
		☐
		☐
		☐
		☐
		☐
		☐
		☐
		☐
		☐
		☐
		☐
		☐
		☐
		☐
		☐
		☐
		☐

11

STEPPING OUT IN FAITH

"Everything you've ever wanted is on the other side of fear."

~ GEORGE ADAIR

WHAT IS YOUR THEME WORD FOR THE YEAR? _____

REFLECT ON YOUR THEME WORD. WHAT DO YOU THINK THIS WORD WILL REQUIRE YOU TO DO DURING THE YEAR?

COMMIT TO STEPPING OUTSIDE IN FAITH AT LEAST ONCE A MONTH FOR THREE MONTHS. WRITE DOWN ONE FAITH-BUILDING ACTIVITY FOR EACH THE NEXT 3 MONTHS AND SET A DEADLINE. DO EACH ACTIVITY BY THE DEADLINE AND THEN RECORD HOW EACH ACTIVITY MADE YOU FEEL AND THE LESSONS YOU LEARNED.

FAITH BUILDING ACTIVITY #1   **DEADLINE**   **DONE**

☐

COMPLETING THIS ACTIVITY MADE ME FEEL:

THIS ACTIVITY TAUGHT ME:

FAITH BUILDING ACTIVITY #2

DEADLINE   **DONE**

☐

COMPLETING THIS ACTIVITY MADE ME FEEL:

THIS ACTIVITY TAUGHT ME:

FAITH BUILDING ACTIVITY #3

DEADLINE   **DONE**

☐

COMPLETING THIS ACTIVITY MADE ME FEEL:

THIS ACTIVITY TAUGHT ME:

40 Days of Miracles

Commit to making room for miracles for the next 40 days, then watch as they flow into your life. Record the miracles here as they occur. Each night, give thanks for your daily miracle(s).

Your miracles could be as profound as getting a check in the mail when you needed it, healed of an illness, or as simple as finding a book or piece of jewelry that you lost. Miracles are everywhere when you are looking!

Miracles on Day 1

_____

_____

Miracles on Day 2

_____

_____

Miracles on Day 3

_____

_____

Miracles on Day 4

_____

_____

Miracles on Day 5

_____

_____

MIRACLES ON DAY 6

_____

···

···

MIRACLES ON DAY 7

···

···

_____

MIRACLES ON DAY 8

···

_____

···

MIRACLES ON DAY 9

_____

···

_____

MIRACLES ON DAY 10

···

···

_____

MIRACLES ON DAY 11

_____

_____

MIRACLES ON DAY 12

_____

_____

MIRACLES ON DAY 13

_____

_____

MIRACLES ON DAY 14

_____

_____

MIRACLES ON DAY 15

_____

_____

MIRACLES ON DAY 16

_____

_____

_____

MIRACLES ON DAY 17

_____

_____

_____

MIRACLES ON DAY 18

_____

_____

_____

MIRACLES ON DAY 19

_____

_____

_____

MIRACLES ON DAY 20

_____

_____

_____

MIRACLES ON DAY 21

_____

_____

MIRACLES ON DAY 22

_____

_____

MIRACLES ON DAY 23

_____

_____

MIRACLES ON DAY 24

_____

_____

MIRACLES ON DAY 25

_____

_____

MIRACLES ON DAY 26

_____

_____

_____

MIRACLES ON DAY 27

_____

_____

_____

MIRACLES ON DAY 28

_____

_____

_____

MIRACLES ON DAY 29

_____

_____

_____

MIRACLES ON DAY 30

_____

_____

_____

MIRACLES ON DAY 31

_____

_____

_____

MIRACLES ON DAY 32

_____

_____

_____

MIRACLES ON DAY 33

_____

_____

_____

MIRACLES ON DAY 34

_____

_____

_____

MIRACLES ON DAY 35

_____

_____

_____

MIRACLES ON DAY 36

_____

_____

_____

MIRACLES ON DAY 37

_____

_____

_____

MIRACLES ON DAY 38

_____

_____

_____

MIRACLES ON DAY 39

_____

_____

_____

MIRACLES ON DAY 40

_____

_____

_____

12

YOUR TIME IS NOW!

"The journey of a thousand miles

begins with one step."

~ LAO TZU

REFLECT ON A TIME WHERE YOU HAD TO WAIT FOR SOMETHING YOU WANTED. WHAT LESSONS DID YOU LEARN WHILE WAITING? WERE THE REWARDS BETTER THAN YOU EXPECTED?

WHAT ARE YOU CURRENTLY WAITING FOR? PRAY OR MEDITATE ON SOME ACTIVITIES THAT WILL PREPARE YOU TO RECEIVE WHAT YOU'RE WAITING FOR AND WRITE THEM DOWN.

MAKE AN ACTION PLAN FOR THE NEXT 30 DAYS. HOW YOU WILL TAKE ACTION ON WHAT YOU'VE LEARNED IN UNSTOPPABLE INFLUENCE? COMPILE ALL OF THE ACTION STEPS YOU WILL TAKE INTO ONE MASTER LIST, THEN PRIORITIZE THE LIST (WITH 1 BEING THE MOST URGENT), ASSIGN DATES AND GET THEM ON YOUR CALENDAR!

ACTION ITEM	PRIORITY	DEADLINE	DONE
Hire a Coach	1	Dec 1	☑
			☐
			☐
			☐
			☐
			☐
			☐
			☐
			☐
			☐
			☐
			☐
			☐
			☐
			☐
			☐
			☐
			☐

PART II

TRANSFORM LIVES

13

FIND YOUR VOICE AND MESSAGE

"You can't find your voice if you don't use it."

~ AUSTIN KLEON

Be bold and commit to doing at least 10 things that make you "uncomfortable" over the next 90 days. Check them off as you complete them and inspire us by sharing your stories at UnstoppableInfluence.com/group

ACTIVITY	DONE
Speaking in public at a meeting	☑
	☐
	☐
	☐
	☐
	☐
	☐
	☐
	☐
	☐
	☐
	☐
	☐
	☐
	☐
	☐
	☐

101 Days to Finding Your Voice.

Place an X in the box for each day that you shoot a video or record a Facebook Live!

1	☐	27	☐	53	☐	79	☐
2	☐	28	☐	54	☐	80	☐
3	☐	29	☐	55	☐	81	☐
4	☐	30	☐	56	☐	82	☐
5	☐	31	☐	57	☐	83	☐
6	☐	32	☐	58	☐	84	☐
7	☐	33	☐	59	☐	85	☐
8	☐	34	☐	60	☐	86	☐
9	☐	35	☐	61	☐	87	☐
10	☐	36	☐	62	☐	88	☐
11	☐	37	☐	63	☐	89	☐
12	☐	38	☐	64	☐	90	☐
13	☐	39	☐	65	☐	91	☐
14	☐	40	☐	66	☐	92	☐
15	☐	41	☐	67	☐	93	☐
16	☐	42	☐	68	☐	94	☐
17	☐	43	☐	69	☐	95	☐
18	☐	44	☐	70	☐	96	☐
19	☐	45	☐	71	☐	97	☐
20	☐	46	☐	72	☐	98	☐
21	☐	47	☐	73	☐	99	☐
22	☐	48	☐	74	☐	100	☐
23	☐	49	☐	75	☐	101	☐
24	☐	50	☐	76	☐		
25	☐	51	☐	77	☐		
26	☐	52	☐	78	☐		

PERFECTLY IMPERFECT

"Always be a first-rate version of yourself,

instead of a second-rate version of somebody else."

~ JUDY GARLAND

REFLECT ON THE STORY YOU WROTE IN CHAPTER 3. WHAT ELSE NEEDS TO BE ADDED TO YOUR STORY? HOW CAN YOUR STORY HELP OTHERS?

WHAT LESSONS CAN SOMEONE TAKE FROM HEARING YOUR STORY?

NOW THAT YOU'VE WRITTEN YOUR STORY. IT'S TIME TO EMBRACE YOUR PERFECTLY IMPERFECT SELF AND RECORD A FACEBOOK LIVE VIDEO. TELL THE WORLD WHO YOU ARE AND WHAT YOU DO. ADD THE HASHTAG #UNSTOPPABLEINFLUENCER TO THE END THEN SHARE IT IN THE UNSTOPPABLE INFLUENCE GROUP AT: *UnstoppableInfluence.com/group*

WHO WILL YOU SERVE?

"The meaning of life is to find your gift.

The purpose of life is to give it away."

~ PICASSO

WHO DO YOU ENJOY WORKING WITH? WHO CAN BENEFIT THE MOST FROM YOUR GIFTS?

WRITE OUT YOUR PERFECT CLIENT STORY USING THE TEMPLATE AT
NatashaHazlett.com/template

IT'S NOT ABOUT YOU!

"You gain strength, courage and confidence by every experience in which you really stop to look fear in the face. You must do the thing you think you cannot do."

~ ELEANOR ROOSEVELT

Make a list of your gifts and then reflect on whether you're sharing them as much and as often as you should be. If not, commit to leveling up your game so you can make a greater impact.

What beliefs or situations may be holding you back? What steps can you take to overcome these perceived challenges?

Belief/Situation	I Can Overcome By
Technology is not my friend	Sign up for local class on how to start a blog
Judy always trash talks my business	Limit my time with Judy

Over the next 30 days, take one personal growth action step each day to become a better you. Read for five minutes, listen to a podcast, watch a web class, attend a workshop, or step outside your comfort zone. Record your activity below.

1	2	3	4	5
Read Unstoppable Influence				
6	7	8	9	10
11	12	13	14	15
16	17	18	19	20
21	22	23	24	25
26	27	28	29	30

17

HOW WILL YOU SERVE?

There's no one alive, that's youer than you!"

~ DR. SEUSS

How will you serve your audience?

WHO ELSE IS SERVING YOUR AUDIENCE? HOW WILL YOUR UNIQUE INFLUENCER PROPOSITION ENCOURAGE BUYERS TO DO BUSINESS WITH YOU?

WRITE DOWN 3-5 IDEAS THAT HAVE COME TO YOU IN THIS CHAPTER.

18

LET'S TALK ABOUT MONEY, HONEY!

> *"Money isn't the most important thing in life,*
> *but it's reasonably close to oxygen*
> *on the 'gotta have it' scale."*
>
> ~ ZIG ZIGLAR

MONEY IS…

WHEN I HAVE MONEY…

If you're a business owner, review your current prices. Are you charging what your products and/or services are really worth? If not, list the reasons below. For each reason determine if the source is Truth or Ego. After completing the exercise, commit to raising your prices, if necessary, so they align with their worth.

ADDITIONAL MONEY BLOCK-BUSTING RESOURCES

Think & Grow Rich by Napoleon Hill

You Are A Badass At Making Money by Jen Sincero

Sacred Success by Barbara Stanny

You Were Born Rich by Bob Proctor

Check out additional resources at: UnstoppableInfluence.com/store

19

MONETIZE YOUR MESSAGE

"The world will pay you exactly what you bargain for. Your rewards will always be in exact proportion to your service. Do you ask for a lot? If so, you will get a lot. Do you ask for a little? If so, you will get a little."

~ EARL NIGHTINGALE

20

UNLEASH YOUR INFLUENCE AND AMPLIFY YOUR MESSAGE

"The ones who are crazy enough to think they can change the world are the ones who do."

~ STEVE JOBS

MAKE A LIST OF THE STORIES YOU'VE TOLD YOURSELF ABOUT THE FOUR TOOLS DISCUSSED IN THIS CHAPTER (WEBSITE, EMAIL LIST, SOCIAL MEDIA, SALES/MARKETING FUNNEL). NEXT TO EACH STORY, DECIDE WHETHER IT'S TRUE OR FALSE. IF THE STORY IS FALSE, CREATE A NEW STORY TO TAKE ITS PLACE.

STORY	TOOL	TRUE/FALSE
I have to share everything	Social Media	False

HOW DO YOUR PRODUCTS OR SERVICES CHANGE PEOPLE'S LIVES?

AUTOMATION TOOLS

Autoresponder

- ✧ MailChimp: Go to NatashaHazlett.com/chimp to set up a FREE account
- ✧ Aweber: Go to NatashaHazlett.com/aweber to get a Free 30-Day Trial

Website Hosting:

- ✧ Hostgator: NatashaHazlett.com/host

Sales & Marketing Automation

- ✧ Our Go-To Platform is ClickFunnels: Go to NatashaHazlett.com/click to get a FREE 14-Day Trial
- ✧ Other Solutions (although not as robust as ClickFunnels)
  - ✧ Infusionsoft
  - ✧ LeadPages

Social Media Platforms

Facebook.com
This popular social media site allows you to connect with friends, family and acquaintances all over the world through posts, status updates, personalized groups and photo sharing.

YouTube.com
YouTube is a video-hosting website that allows you to both store and serve video content. Users can post, view or share videos that have been uploaded.

Twitter.com
Considered a "microblogging" service, Twitter allows you to share short posts and share pictures. The posts, or Tweets as they have been coined, are limited to 140 characters. You can like, "re-tweet" (share) or comment under any post.

LinkedIn.com
A professional social media designed specifically for the business community. LinkedIn allows you to list important career milestones, project details and business affiliates while connecting with other professionals within your industry.

Pinterest.com
Pinterest is a social media platform where you can upload, store and share images which are called, "pins". These pins can then be added to a, "pinboard" which can be sorted into various genres and followed by other Pinterest members.

Instagram.com
Instagram enables you to upload pictures and short videos through computers and a mobile app. Content can be "liked" shared or commented on by other users. Hashtags and geo tags allow users to easily search for relevant for location specific content.

SnapChat.com
Snapchat is a mobile app where you can both send and receive photos, short videos and messages. The recipient has 10 seconds to view the content before it disappears.

Outsource/Freelance Resources

Upwork.com
Upwork is an international freelancing platform allowing you to post jobs and prospective candidates to search for a job based on their skills and experience.

Fiverr.com
Fiverr provides you with the option to choose from over 3 million a la carte services which are called, "Gigs" These services can be purchased for as low as $5 or as high as $500. You can use it for graphics, web services, transcription, voice overs, just to name a few services found on the site.

UNSTOPPABLE
I N F L U E N C E

YOU'RE INVITED!

It's time to Be You. Be Fearless & Transform Lives! Now that you know the path to take, there's nothing that can stop you now...

Except that loud mouth in your head.

Your busy schedule.

Your friends or family that don't "get it"

I don't want *anything* stopping you from unleashing your influence in the world. I'm on a mission to help you to discover and fulfill your calling, no matter what it is!

The journey to Unstoppable Influence shouldn't be one that you take alone. It's far more exciting and enjoyable when you can link arms with like-minded Influencers.

So, I want to invite you to join my private community and get all of the tools and strategies you need to boost your influence (and income) this year, *without working longer hours.*

You can find out more at <u>UnstoppableInfluence.com/class</u>

ABOUT NATASHA

Natasha Nassar Hazlett is best known as a Personal Brand Strategist. She empowers entrepreneurs around the world with the clarity, confidence, and strategies they need to boost their income and influence while working less, by monetizing their message online.

In addition to being a mentor and coach, Natasha is a speaker, award-winning internet marketer, practicing attorney, and the cofounder of Fast Forward Marketing, LLC with her husband Rich. Most importantly, though, she's mom to an adorable little girl.

She is also the creator of the *Savvy Business Blueprint*™. *The Idaho Business Review* honored Natasha with their 2013 Idaho Women of the Year award, and she has been honored multiple times with the Rising Star Award by *Super Lawyers* magazine.

You can learn more about Natasha at: NatashaHazlett.com and connect with her on social media at:

Facebook: NatashaHazlett.com/FB
Instagram: NatashaHazlett.com/IG
YouTube: NatashaHazlett.com/YT

Made in the USA
Middletown, DE
05 February 2019